Murfles and

Wink-a-peeps

FUNNY OLD WORDS FOR KIDS

by Susan Kelz Sperling

drawings by Tom Bloom

CLARKSON N. POTTER, INC. / PUBLISHERS, NEW YORK

Distributed by Crown Publishers, Inc.

With lip-claps for my younger poplollies,
JANE, STUART, MATTHEW,
and DUKE
S. K. S.

.   .   .

For my very own bellibone,
KATHLEEN
T. B.

Text copyright © 1985 by Susan Kelz Sperling
Illustrations copyright © 1985 by Tom Bloom

Published by Clarkson N. Potter, Inc., One Park Avenue,
New York, New York 10016 and simultaneously in Canada by
General Publishing Company Limited

Manufactured in Italy

CLARKSON N. POTTER, POTTER, and colophon are trademarks of
Clarkson N. Potter, Inc.

Typography by Kathleen Westray

Library of Congress Cataloging in Publication Data
Sperling, Susan Kelz.   Murfles and wink-a-peeps.
Summary: Presents more than sixty obsolete words that are now seldom
or never used, such as "flap-dragon" and "muckender,"
and includes poems and a list of names to call people.
1. English language—Obsolete words—Juvenile literature.
2. Vocabulary—Juvenile literature. [1. English language—
Obsolete words.   2. Vocabulary] I. Bloom, Tom, ill.   II. Title.
PE1667.S59   1985   428.1   85-6274
ISBN 0-517-55659-6

10 9 8 7 6 5 4 3 2 1

First Edition

Dear Boonfellows,

Do the words *murfles* and *wink-a-peeps* sound strange to you? More than two hundred or so years ago, when your grandmother's grandmother's grandmother was alive, they simply meant "freckles" and "eyes."

The reason *murfles* and *wink-a-peeps* are not familiar to you is that they are old English words that are no longer used and cannot be found in most current dictionaries.

How did these words die? All words, even today, are constantly going through a kind of popularity contest. Many words disappear when other words having similar meanings come along and take their places. *Murfles* and *wink-a-peeps* are only two of the thousands of words used long ago that gradually lost their popularity and are no longer included in conversations, books, and dictionaries.

A word may also die if it describes a custom or thing that has disappeared. Once upon a time, *flap-dragon* was a dangerous stunt performed by knights to impress their ladies. A cup filled with brandy, bits of bread, and raisins was set on fire. When a knight drank this strange mixture, it felt as if a dragon were flapping its fiery tongue at him. Because that custom died, so did the word *flap-dragon*. If some of the things we use today disappear, so will the words that describe them. A few hundred years from now, *sneakers, yo-yo,* and *bubble gum* might sound as strange as *flap-dragon.*

Sometimes the pronunciations and spellings of words change as they are being used. Many years after appearing one way, words may be spoken and written differently from the way they were originally. For example, today's word *freaks* may be related to the rare word *reaks,* which was popular in the late 1500s and meant "tricks" or "jokes." Somehow an *f* was added as the first letter and the word's whole appearance changed.

Muckender, meaning "handkerchief" or "bib," also underwent a few changes in spelling. In the late 1400s it was spelled *mokedore,* and a hundred years later it became *mucketter.* Soon after that, the word changed to *muckender* and stayed that way for two hundred years more before it passed out of use.

This book presents more than sixty lost words that are seldom or never used. Some of these long-lost words are fun to look at and to say aloud. Some have interesting meanings and combinations of letters. Others seem modern enough to be used today.

I have combined many of these old words with modern English to create seven rounds. Each round presents five of the words, one at a time, and repeats the first word at the end of the round to make a circle of words.

I have also included some of the words in poems. And there's even a list of names to call people.

I hope you enjoy the sights and sounds of these lost words. Feel free to borrow as many as you like. Try· them out on your friends and see if they can figure out what you're saying.

Have fun, and spread the word!

S.K.S.

Glopping and Pingling

What is glop?

Glop means to swallow greedily. When you're really hungry, you can hardly wait to glop your bellytimber.

What is bellytimber?

Bellytimber is food. Healthful bellytimber keeps you strong but lubber-wort does not.

What is lubber-wort?

Lubber-wort is junk food. Eating too much lubber-wort can make you feel very sloomy.

. . .

What is sloomy?

Sloomy means lazy and sleepy. Sloomy people often pingle at mealtime.

What is pingle?

Pingle means to eat with very little appetite. The vegetables you might pingle over, a more greedy person will happily glop.

Dizzy Doings

What is a whistersnefet?

A whistersnefet is a slap on the ear. A strong whistersnefet can make you very turngiddy.

. . .

What is turngiddy?

Turngiddy means dizzy. Some people get turngiddy at the top of a downsteepy hill.

What is downsteepy?

Downsteepy means steep or slanted. Go slowly on any downsteepy road that leads into a dingle.

What is a dingle?

A dingle is a valley between hills. Farmers who live in dingles yerd their cows to get them back into the barn.

What is yerd?

Yerd means to poke with a stick. A good friend would never yerd you or give you a whistersnefet.

Puzzling Questions

What is a hufty-tufty?

A hufty-tufty is a show-off who likes to brag, especially about the reaks he plays on people.

What are reaks?

Reaks are jokes or tricks, like hiding someone's shoes in a flosh.

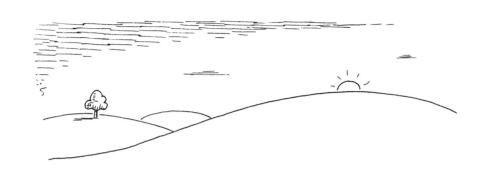

What is a flosh?

A flosh is a swamp filled with tangled weeds. Frogs in a flosh seem to croak more loudly at dimpse than at other times.

. . .

What is dimpse?

Dimpse is twilight, the time when day turns into night, and a fopdoodle might lose his way home.

. . .

What is a fopdoodle?

A fopdoodle is a fool. Admitting he is a fopdoodle is something a hufty-tufty would never do.

Sights and Sounds

What are ataballes?

Ataballes are kettledrums. Playing the ataballes very loudly can make a room quop with sound.

. . .

What is quop?

Quop means to throb or beat. A compliment on her clothing is sure to make a prickmedainty's heart quop with pride.

. . .

What is a prickmedainty?

A prickmedainty is a fancy, fussy dresser who always wears the latest in stylish clothes. A prickmedainty would find it teenful if no one noticed her new outfit.

What is teenful?

Teenful means irritating or annoying. It must be teenful for a person to get food caught in his bugle-beard.

What is a bugle-beard?

A bugle-beard is a shaggy beard that is soft and fluffy. A musician with a long bugle-beard needs to be careful that it doesn't get in the way when he's playing the ataballes.

All Around Your Face

What is croodle?

Croodle means to hum or sing quietly. Early in the morning you can hear the birds croodle, even before you open your wink-a-peeps.

What are wink-a-peeps?

Wink-a-peeps are eyes. It's time to visit the barber when your crinets fall into your wink-a-peeps.

What are crinets?

Crinets are hair. People with red crinets usually have a lot of murfles.

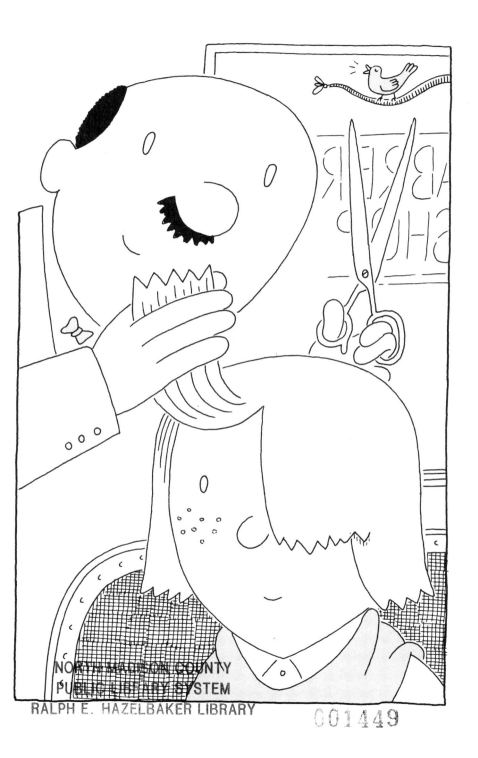

What are murfles?

Murfles are freckles. Some people think that murfles appear wherever the sun plants little lip-claps.

What are lip-claps?

Lip-claps are kisses. Isn't it nice to tuck a baby into bed with lip-claps and croodle a lullaby?

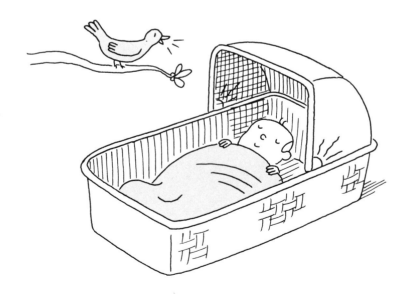

Special Things

What is a poplolly?

A poplolly is someone you like a lot, someone you think is very special. On Valentine's Day it's nice to surprise your poplolly with a tuzzy-muzzy.

What is a tuzzy-muzzy?

A tuzzy-muzzy is a bouquet of flowers. A pretty tuzzy-muzzy brightens up a dark cosh.

. . .

What is a cosh?

A cosh is a small cottage. Next to his cosh a farmer might build a barn with a boose.

. . .

What is a boose?

A boose is the stall where an animal lives. A boose is a fine place to keep your blonke.

. . .

What is a blonke?

A blonke is a horse, usually a hardworking one. Sometimes a blonke is such a good friend it deserves to be called a poplolly.

Funny Situations

What is a ha-ha?

A ha-ha is a ditch a person doesn't notice until he falls into it. It's not nice to snirtle at someone who lands in a ha-ha.

What is snirtle?

Snirtle means to snicker or laugh at. Halloween brings lots of chances to snirtle at people who wear farture under their costumes.

What is farture?

Farture is stuffing. A sharp flatchet can easily rip through pillows and send farture and feathers flying all over the place.

What is a flatchet?

A flatchet is a sword. A knight might have kept a flatchet handy under his bedroom eyethurl in case of a sudden attack.

What is an eyethurl?

An eyethurl is a window. You never know when
you might be idly gazing out of your eyethurl
and see someone accidentally trip into a ha-ha.

⊡⊡ I Can Count Your Murfles
(Bet You Can't Count Mine)

I can count your murfles,   freckles
(Bet you can't count mine);
That's 'cause you have just a few,
But I have twenty-nine.

Or as many as four hundred,
They're sparpled everywhere!   scattered
At night I lie upon my donge   mattress
And think, "Who put them there?"

Food for Thought

What's your favorite bellytimber?   food
Do you always glop your cake?   swallow greedily
Get sloomy at the dinner table?   lazy, sleepy
Pingle over fish or steak?   eat with little appetite

Is lubber-wort, like chips and soda,   junk food
The only stuff you like to stuff?
As for me, all food tastes yummy,
I can never get enough!

I Saw Two Malshaves Lip-clapping

I saw two malshaves   caterpillars
   lip-clapping   kissing
On top of a zuche's leaf;   tree stump
I knew I shouldn't be watching,
But the sight was beyond belief!

I heard two malshaves lip-clapping,
Making such a sound
Of chomping, brooling, slurping,   soft humming
While I lay on the ground.

I left those malshaves lip-clapping,
While mally did they stay;   affectionate, fond
I put on my coat and nabcheat,   cap
And quietly tiptoed away.

Best Boonfellows

My dog and I are boonfellows,   friends
He's more fun than a circus rubb.   seal
He loves to have his crinets brushed,   hair
When he's all finished with his tub.

If he stepped on a tingle-nail,   small tack
While we were walking in the wong,   meadow
I'd bandage up his wounded paw,
And croodle him a soothing song.   sing quietly

His wink-a-peeps gaze up at me,   eyes
"Come play some reaks," he seems   tricks
    to say;
He'll always be my poplolly,   special loved one
I'll love him till he's old and gray.

Brothers and Sisters

Oh what a shock did Liza have
When scrogglings roared on her   rotten apples
   like thunder!
Because her little brother Billy
Flerked the tree branch she   jerked, shook
   was under.

"Barlafumble!" didn't stop   a cry meaning "stop!"
   him,
Flesh-spades were her only choice.   fingernails
And so they brangled, Liza winning,   argued
And Billy, shouting, lost his voice.

Moe MacDougal

Moe MacDougal danced a jig,
And landed on his ribbled pig;   wrinkled

The pig was carked by such   annoyed, alarmed
   a scare,
It threw MacDougal in the air;

Moe grabbed a star and hung on tight,
His fingers quopped throughout   throbbed
   the night;

Until he caught a passing cloud,
And, bloring down to earth,   shouting, bellowing
   he vowed,

"No more fadoodle for silly me!   nonsense
I'll plan my darg beneath a tree!"   day's work

pretty poplolly

silly fopdoodle

favorite bellibone

goofy fleak

wacky fizgig

special loved one

fool

lovely girl

scatterbrain

dizzy person

fopdoodle

rutterkin

poplolly

hufty-tufty

dopey velvet-head	idiot
warm fellowfeeler	sympathizer
dumb fonkin	clowning person
grabby greediguts	glutton
stuck-up hufty-tufty	show-off
loyal aimcrier	supporter, encourager
yucky yisser	envious person
prissy prickmedainty	fussy, fancy dresser
bragging rutterkin	bully
true boonfellow	good friend
sneaky blob-tale	tattletale

Glossary

a. adjective
n. noun
v. verb

aimcrier n., a supporter, an encourager

ataballes n., kettledrums

barlafumble n., a cry meaning "stop," "halt," or "time out"

bellibone n., a lovely girl, both pretty and good

bellytimber n., food

blob-tale n., a tattletale

blonke n., a hardworking horse

blore v., to shout, bellow

boonfellow n., a friend, companion

boose n., a stall where an animal lives

brangle v., to argue with words and fists

brool v., to hum softly

bugle-beard n., a shaggy beard

carked a., annoyed, alarmed

cosh n., a small cottage

crinets n., hair

croodle v., to hum or sing quietly

darg n., a day's work

dimpse n., twilight, time when day turns into night

dingle n., a valley between hills

donge n., a mattress

downsteepy a., steep, slanted

eyethurl n., a window

fadoodle n., nonsense, silliness

farture n., stuffing

fellowfeeler n., a sympathizer

fizgig n., a dizzy person

flap-dragon n., a dangerous stunt knights performed by drinking from a cup filled with flaming brandy, bits of bread, and raisins

flatchet *n.*, a sword
fleak *n.*, a scatterbrain
flerk *v.*, to jerk or shake
flesh-spades *n.*, fingernails
flosh *n.*, a swamp filled with tangled weeds
fonkin *n.*, a clowning person
fopdoodle *n.*, a fool

glop *v.*, to swallow greedily
greediguts *n.*, a glutton, greedy person

ha-ha *n.*, a ditch a person doesn't notice until he falls into it
hufty-tufty *n.*, a show-off, bragging person

lip-clap *n.*, a kiss
lubber-wort *n.*, junk food

mally *a.*, affectionate, fond
malshave *n.*, a caterpillar
murfles *n.*, freckles

nabcheat *n.*, a cap, small hat

pingle *v.*, to eat with very little appetite
poplolly *n.*, a special loved one
prickmedainty *n.*, a fancy, fussy dresser

quop *v.*, to throb, beat

reak *n.*, a trick, joke
ribbled *a.*, wrinkled
rubb *n.*, a seal
rutterkin *n.*, a bully

scroggling *n.*, a rotten apple left on tree after harvest
sloomy *a.*, lazy, sleepy
snirtle *v.*, to snicker or laugh at
sparpled *a.*, scattered

teenful *a.*, irritating, annoying
tingle-nail *n.*, a small tack
turngiddy *a.*, dizzy
tuzzy-muzzy *n.*, a bouquet of flowers

velvet-head *n.*, a dumb, dopey person, an idiot

whistersnefet *n.*, a slap on the ear
wink-a-peeps *n.*, eyes
wong *n.*, a meadow

yerd *v.*, to poke with a stick
yisser *n.*, an envious person

zuche *n.*, a tree stump